I KNOW ABOUT THESE THINGS

I KNOW ABOUT THESE THINGS

POEMS BY

CYNTHIA JACOBI

Library of Congress Control Number: 2025900986

ISBN 978-1-7373958-6-7
Turnstone Books of Oregon, LLC
Seal Rock, Oregon
Logo courtesy of Pepper Trail

For my daughter, Valerie

Acknowledgments:

Poems previously appeared in:

Tuesday: Volume 6, 2012
"Arrowhead Lake, Minnesota"
"Crime Scene"
"How to Clean Your Steps"
"Nye Beach Walk"

Tuesday: Volume 7, 2013
"Family Style"
"Telephone Connection: Information Please"

Concord:
"Photo at Silver Lake 1947"
"Poets"
"Pill Box"

Verseweavers 2013
"Iris Inominata". first place
"Tribe" third place

Verseweavers 2015
"Un-doing". Hon Mem.
"It's a Beautiful Bridge". Third place

Verseweavers 2018
"Territory". Hon Mention

Verseweavers 2019
"My Selfie Poem". Third place

Verseweavers 2021
"Musings in a Seaside Garden". Hon Mention
"A Gratitude". Third place

North Coast Squid
"The Aquarium"
"To Be Strong and Swift"

Stealing Time
"The Quickening"

Mortality Poems, 2024
"Chemotherapy: Week 8"
"Mercy for My Mother, or Regrets for My Late Arrival"

The Grace of Oregon Rain, 2024
"Weather Forecast"

CONTENTS

The Fortune

She cracked open crisp folds
to behold her paper fortune:
"Have patience with everything
unsolved in your heart."

The Look of Poets

I love the look of poets–
from published sophisticates
to those who live on little but wit
from those who appear totally aware
to those who are slightly awake
wearing tailored jackets or rumpled denim
in cowboy boots or barefoot with ponytails
unwilling to contain electrified hair.

I love the poets whose task it is to ask
those questions which connect and tether us.

I love the sound of poets' voices
speaking their words while
receivers murmur hmmmm
as leaves rustling in acknowledgment.

I love the work of poets when
writing that one best poem
changes every cell in your body.

Candy in His Pocket, or He Went to Algeria

Always on Saturday morning
Grandpa wore a plaid flannel shirt
with candy in his pocket.
He spooned hot coffee into a saucer
adding a splash of milk
and sprinkle of sugar.
Just let it cool off a bit he said
eyes winking behind round gold frames.
I lapped like a cat.
Grandma frowned at us
her dentures clicking
worried about coffee and my bad habits.

A machinist by trade
Grandpa got through the Depression
never losing the house
the source of extra money unspoken.

Grandpa came late for dinner
tripping up the porch steps
in a cloud of beer fumes
eating his cold pork chops
and onions alone.

He showed me framed photos
of solemn ancestors–
one of his mother
in dappled woods near Warsaw,
another of his brother Pierre
a French Foreign Legion soldier
on horseback, cloaked in white.

He went to Algeria.
I came to America.

Sanctuary

Just below the bump of purple vein
  she kept a hankie tucked at the top
  of her knee-high nylons, left leg.
Her right hand could keep on doing
  what it needed to do–
  stir the pot or open the door
while, with the left hand, she could catch
  a sneeze, dry a tear, dab a nose.
Both arms together were sanctuary
   soft footfalls of her heart against my ear.
One Easter Sunday, she posed under naked oaks
  with her sisters, crowned
  by floral hats and sunshine
  her hankie fluttered under a polka-dot hem.

Forget Me Not

Gran's seated beneath the Tiffany shade
light focused on her neat head,
hair pinned and bunned.
Amber glow warmed her pale skin
always protected as Victorian lady she was.
Soft gold gleamed on her wedding band
worn thin from fifty years of a tired marriage.
Lilac talc powdered her neck.
She wore a dainty floral dress
of sky-blue Forget-Me-Nots
with her left pocket forever empty
over a breast no more.

A Vintage Photo from Tampa

The woman's eyes are squinting
from the Florida sunshine
A small girl at her side gazes upwards
A plump bow in her curled hair
A lunch pail in her grasp
The woman swollen with pregnancy
leans against an aluminum screen door
Cigarette in her hand
Long ash ready to rain
Onto pretty heads
Of potted marigolds

Laundry Queen Photo

Her glance is sealed in fading sepia.
She looks back and down over her shoulder
   lips closed, barely smiling
   serene and queenly, wind fluffing her hair.
She was about to reach down into the
   wicker basket of wet laundry and clothes pins
   to add parallel lines of
   cumulus sheets and cirrus diapers
   snowdrops of socks and
   daisy chains of underwear
   to dry and freshen in the sun.
I puzzled why Father would want
   these photos of Mother hanging laundry.
She wore a white blouse and gingham skirt
   her bared arms strong.
She stood on tip-toe, feet in strappy sandals,
   southern breeze lifting her skirt
   outlining her legs.

Family Style

Pottery bowls squatted full on the table
Jane's paisley cloth under their warm rounded bottoms
Grandma's Japanese trivet gripped the gravy boat
dishes were passed to the left
Uncle Jim and his two boys dove into the noodles
   out of turn as expected
opinions wove into gossip
   topics forbidden were salaries, Grandpa's will,
   or the whereabouts of our cousin Paul
Although they could be kind and generous
   this family had no culture for words of love
little ones did not hear
   good night I love you sweet precious
and so did not know
how to speak love later to their own
this family cheerfully nattered on
   speculating endlessly–
   who went where and when and why
   who should sweep their own alleys
   why Katzie married Ted with no hope of
   her own child since Ted had suffered mumps
   causing undescended testicles
but they did not speak of love

Crime Scene

I waited in line
almost tall enough
to reach the counter.

I ordered two wieners and a coke.
I sat with my aunt and we ate.
How disgusting, she snorted.
Suddenly ashamed, I looked at
ketchup dribbles on my shirt.
Terrible! It's a cardinal sin—never forget that.

She pointed. My eyes followed her finger
toward the next people waiting in line.
They were holding hands
one black and one white.

A Child's Christmas in Denver

With a loud Ho Ho Ho
Santa came into our house
his red suit smelled of mothballs
his beard looked funny
Santa had Father's voice
two big elves were with him
they were going bowling
Santa laughed Father's laugh
he and the elves took drinks from
shiny flat bottles in their pockets
then went outside
into the snow singing and shouting

A loud crash woke me
I peeked 'round the corner
Mother sat silent in her reading chair
with the light on
our Christmas tree lay
sideways on the floor
broken glass ornaments at her feet
Santa was asleep
his head in his plate of cookies
by the fireplace where
he'd fallen down the chimney

The Cellar

The children wouldn't go to the cellar
Where the coal furnace lived
Its wide square mouth filled
With chipped black teeth
Metal octopus arms stretching
High into every room
Where children slept
Blowing hot fire breath
Into their dreams

How to Clean Your Steps

In Holland, Mother said, the housewives
wash their steps with milk.
When buckets clatter empty
the cats come, mewing in excited stutters.
They scour the steps,
rough, pink tongues seeking milk.
Purring, they sprawl onto their thin ribs,
rolling back to side, over and over
pressing their fur into the steps
buffing the stones to a pearly sheen.

Finding Orion

Three white stars glowed on the front
wheel fork, handlebars trailed tassels
plump fat tires wobbled

when Father took off the training
wheels. I pedaled on
as he ran beside me

We sat on the porch at dusk
eating Dreamsicles to celebrate
my flight on two wheels

Pale yellow lantern house lights
began to warm the dark
We guessed the night sounds:

car engine, door slamming
cat mew or baby cry?
whisper of bat wings

voices calling for Trixie
the scratch of gophers digging
spiders weaving webs

On this night he taught me to find
Orion, Hunter of the skies, his shining
belt studded by three white stars

Arrowhead Lake, Minnesota

We stopped at Olson's for ice, minnows,
A couple of beers for my Dad,
And new adult license for me –
The sixteen-year-old girl-woman.

We loaded our gear into a rented boat.
He started the motor and chugged to
Our lucky Salad Bowl hole.
I baited a jerking minnow onto my hook.

I cast out just as he taught me.
My hands felt a long, heavy tug
Followed by slow bucking
Which spoke Walleye language.

We caught our limit–
Cleaned and iced four silvery fish
Ate cupcakes and then ate sandwiches and pickles
Headed home in thickening blue dusk.

I knew he wanted to ask about
The dark-haired boy who drove slowly
Past our house and then
Squealed tires at the corner.

I turned away, silent, staring at the night road.
I could see distant red tail lights bobbing,
Bobbing in and out of
Darkened birch forest.

To Be Strong and Swift

The blonde girl yearned to be an Indian Princess
with dark braids down to her waist,
a quiver of blue-feathered arrows on her shoulder.
She wanted to ride a Palomino pony bareback,
strong and swift through the forest,
wind whipping those braids straight back,
her fingers buried in silky mane.
She wanted to do rodeo tricks standing up to applause
with silver bracelets jingling
later palming windfall apples into a velvet muzzle
pony breath warming her hand.
She sauntered to school, her backpack balanced,
a wrapped lunch on top of books
She pulled up her plaid knee socks
always dreaming to be
someone,
somewhere else.

Photo at Silver Lake

Though they had already lived a lifetime,
here they smile, young and fresh.
He–returned by sheer luck from Anzio.
She–nursing in Veteran's Memorial wards.
My tall uncle in a slouch hat, one eye shaded,
His legs so long that his crotch was at her waist.
My aunt,–gazing up–wavy hair clipped
back on one side like Lauren Bacall,
In shorts and saddle shoes, her left knee bent,
looking saucy, one foot half out of her shoe.
Hefting brown bottles of old Schlitz,
They lean into each other,
They adore.

I know now what they could not.
I know of their life well lived with candles at meals,
of a marriage ended with his death preceded
by strokes and marathon rehabs.
If effort were all, he could have raced with Kenyans.
I know about her–miscarriage after miscarriage–
of how she delivered one little bloody inchling
into the toilet and how she saved it for the priest.
I know for both the joy at last of a healthy son.
I know of her final years:
blind and nearly deaf,
she talked to him every day
but couldn't say his name.

To Slip the Surly Bonds of Earth
(After "High Flight," John Magee)

Some fathers make marks in chalk on blackboards.
My father made marks in the sky with a jet plane.
I would watch high above as his tight trails gradually
softened,
releasing vapor patterns into nothingness.

Zipped into his flight suit
Weather report and
Flight assignment in hand
Wearing dark navigator sunglasses
With his helmet thunking against his hip
He kissed mother, then kissed me and my sister
And strode off to do what he loved
Nylon covered legs
Slick, slick, slick against each other
His boots firmly crossing the porch.

In a party room downstairs teens gathered.
A telephone rang. It rang again.
But not for any of us.
The doorbell chimed.
Adults upstairs whispered.

We overheard, and then they told us–
A plane was down and lost.

"Help me, Rhonda help help me Rhonda yeah"
Spun on the turntable,
Needle stuck in the grooves.
My breath felt plastered to my ribs.
"Help me, Rhonda, Help me, Help me."
It seemed no one could look directly at each other.

• • •

There was a soft tapping at the door.
Two blue uniforms stood there, hats in hands.

Trudy, my friend, can you forgive me?
I was happy that it was your father.

Tribe

I am a Tribe of One, the others gone,
cycles complete.

I am Daughter of Grace.
I carry her silence within.

I am grand-daughter of Agneiszka and Marta,
sailor-survivors of Atlantic voyage.

I am great-grand-daughter of Elzbieta,
Karola, and other names now lost,
Dead from birthing.

We all have worn our
cheekbones high, our noses long, perhaps
the gifts from a tall Ukrainian trekking
the Carpathian Mountains
through Polish villages to find farmers
with Potatoes, Doves, and Daughters.

Sedum

These are welcome garden guests
these friendly, squatting sedum.
Flung far from origins in eastern Europe
and western Asia, they are tidy
petals of pale, gray pockets
pastel edged with pink and blue.

I like to think that women in Syria invite
these native succulents to abide
in their gardens, as do I.

Sedum ibericum,
a hermaphrodite, is both
male and female.
Gladly self-fertile, they
may live in solitude yet be open
to pollen from roaming insects.

But we women—
we can't reproduce without
males even if they are the ones who
hide car bombs in Aleppo or
direct drones from
bunkers in Nebraska.

Lovely as a Ginkgo Leaf

She grew tall and gangly
    and linked arms with girlfriends while
    the boys waited for her braces to come off.
She became lovely as a ginkgo leaf
    with elegant stems and soft, ruffled edges.
But lightning could crackle from her lips.
At other times, she yearned
    to lock her arms around her mother.

Mrs. Sikorsky's Parakeet

Bow legged Little Baby skipped
  about his private playground
  wheels bells and seed statues
  tiny round mirrors reflecting turquoise

To be invited for summer lemonade
  meant I could visit Little Baby
  let his claws clasp my finger perch
His feet were cool and smooth, breast feathers soft

I wanted to hold his body between my palms
  not squeezing too hard, you understand,
  just to feel warmth of his body
  and the beat of his bird heart

His bright blue head cocked back and forth
  one black rimmed eye at a time
  as Little Baby assessed me
What are you doing here, little girl?

Blinking Little Baby
  inspected me from a bird's eye view:
  lanky lean boy-hipped
  clear eyed and curious

Little Baby hopped onto Mrs. Sikorsky's finger
She was the only one he would kiss
  chirp and kiss her cheek over and over
I wanted kisses too

So a few summers later
  when I got whispered invitations
  Come kiss me Baby
I did

Love at First Light

The first time I laid eyes on him
There fell a circle of light upon his face
Like a shimmer of star shine
Then he touched me without using his hands
There and there
His eyes so dark I could not look away

The Aquarium

Long tailed guppies float between us.
Neon Tetras school and flash
under tube-light fluorescence,
captives in a contained world
of burbling white noise.
I see your face on the other side
through the glass.
I want to touch you but all this stuff is in the way–
Sand and grit, plastic tubing,
Tinkerbelle mermaids trapped by their tales.
An overflowing treasure chest
spilling coins.
Two miniature castle towers,
moated, water circling
under the bridge.

Endless Season

The next ringing of the
bell seemed light years away
at the start of summer
without school books
an endless season of play

The child in me could not imagine
an end to summer
when fireflies disappeared
like the passing of grandparents
their deaths wrapped in mystery

Now it's summer again
and the solstice has flipped the light
to make longer the nights

The child in me delights in my garden
grooming roses of spent petals

The corn is sweet and tomatoes are ripe
The child in me now knows
Queen Anne cherries are here
but for a brief reign

The child in me has learned
that the bell will ring at the end
of what seems endless

It may be a harsh clang
or soft as fairy chimes
which I may not hear

Secret Follies

With the optimism of young trees
and flower heads turning to follow the sun

With wild creatures in their hearts
and first loves flaming as scarlet roses

They ate peaches upholstered in velvet
and cracked a circus of sunny side up eggs
    into a new pan

They danced on carpets of lamp glow
in purple darkness under star lanes

This was long ago before they carried
    cups quivering in saucers
and silenced secret follies of the heart

Musings in a Seaside Garden

Lavender wands bend with weight of
wandering bees, pine scent wafts in the updraft
I hear overhead the buzz of a clouded plane
the persistent moan of the jetty whistle
I pick lemon verbena for tea thinking of how
it perfumed Southern ladies' linens

Rising sun heats my back
In seep memories of a new baby
a warm curled violin
between my cheek and shoulder
her quick breaths and animal stirrings
waking stretch and a diapered fart
open rose mouth wailing and rooting
milk soaking my dress and her dress
I smell sharp odors of thyme trod underfoot
I see ferns unfurling from caterpillars into fans

Iris Innominata

When the shell of my ear snares chirps
from darting birds with scissored tails
I know that on this day
wild iris will bloom.

Three moon-white petals each,
veined in royal purple
pale yellow jewels in their throats.

My Selfie Poem

I have middle-aged children

I wonder at their infant survival under my care
   and wish I could do it over

My thoughts skip and pause
   as might a yellow pencil
   put to lined paper

I remember a collage of shoes
   lost front teeth
   report cards driving lessons
   first heartbreak

I write free form poetry
   It's playing tennis without a net
   To quote Robert Frost

I must squint to focus
   and focus to be grateful

Starflowers of love returned shimmer
   in my silver hair
I breathe deep with acceptances

I have stashed an egg of barbed wire
   on a high shelf
a chalice of questions without answers

Winter Closet

There are no strangers on the pegged rack

One hat cozy-ed next to another
Knitted scarves drape together
Below, a line of boots stand at attention

This is a house kept tidy
Objects placed with purpose
Pairs matched, clothes on hangers

The snowmen sweaters are packed
With boxed ornaments
Ready for the next year

Here the quilted coats hang in silent suspension
No whispers of sleeve brushing body
A pocket holds flowers of folded tissue
But there by the door
  One mitten has lost her other hand

The Seventh Wave

I found my mother
sitting cross legged in the sand,
ocean lapping at her knees

Approaching, then receding
trailing luminous foam garlands
caressing the flesh of her frail body.

My mother tossed a grey stone,
tumbled smooth, into the water and
breathed a wish.

The tide force turned, swirling,
then drew back,
sucking pain and sorrow.

The Seventh Wave of
churning sea broth filled her lap
with oysters and pearls.

Where I Press My Cheek

My black faux fur
pillow, softly sleek,
still enshrouds molecules
of my Mother's scent–
a contrast between Pall Mall
tobacco–a sharp sweetness
before match strike
flames the cigarette–
and Chanel #5.
Then
I remember how
her freshly curled
Vogue-elegant
hairshape smelled
of *Halo* shampoo.

Oranges

Oranges are there in the memory bank
  I keep for my mother

She showed me how to first dent the dimpled skin
  to release the globe inside

How then to shell the peel slowly saving the flesh
  for perfect separate segments

How to tease away the white membranes
  which could be both bitter and sad

She watched over me from the moment
  I was placed squalling on the altar of her breasts

My orange is peeled
  and perfectly segmented

I eat and taste the sweet acid tingle
I eat alone and taste the sad

The Reluctant Mother

Amid her succession of spaniels and dachshunds
She would say tartly to us
"Have puppies, never children."
She had abandoned her cello and
retired from Gimbel's giftware to give birth four times.
She always fed us, clothed us,
admonished us to properness,
polished us for our public.
My sister reminds me that
each child is born into a different family.
I thought Mother was just tired of Texas and hated the
bugs.
My sister says that Mother drank beer and
couldn't plant the gladiolas right side up.
I told my sister that sometimes she had hugged us
but the camera never caught her holding us except as
anonymous newborns.
Last year at the old house
We found a box marked "SAVE."
She kept the plaster histories of our little handprints,
the teeth exchanged by the Fairy,
and the macaroni necklaces.

Mercy for My Mother,
Regrets for my late arrival

In another time, you might have floated
on a burial pyre into a dark fjord

A proud and honored princess
of a wandering tribe

You left as a candle flame
slow snuffed lacking oxygen

Your passage eased by morphia
bitter drops under the tongue

Gone were green cylinders and tubing
cups, straws, swabs, the to-do list

Your body had been rolled and zipped
into the pre-planned biodegradable bag

The mattress had been washed
rolled and zipped, tossed into a truck

A skeleton bed frame of bare wires
naked coiled springs exposed

Threw shadows of connecting
circles and spirals and crosses

Shaped by your final repose
Knee crank up, head raised

● ● ●

Handwriting

My hand moves as did my mother's.
To be precise, our handwriting is so alike
only we could tell who wrote the message
with a certain swoop on the "t"
the open topped "a"
flat "m" and "n"
identical to a casual observer

I have learned a fresh
and fitting word
for an art form of text: *asemic*
defined as illegible handwriting

More precisely, true *asemic*
handwriting occurs
when the writer cannot read it the next day—
an abstract calligraphy
We practiced this art form for decades.
Yes, *asemic* intuition. Who knew?

Pill Box 1968

A Fiesta pink oblong falls out of the open bin:
the morning dose and a noon dose flashing joyous colors.
Then a blue pill:
a calm globe, casually rolling out of its bottle,
starting its work at bedtime
creating velvet dreams.
Next from a round dispenser:
a disc, pure and white
a tiny plump Host
obligated to suppress ovulation,
destined to change history.

Thanks for leaving

Thank you for leaving to plough your greener pastures.
Thank you for commuting the life sentence
we swore to fulfill in St. Stevens Church,
witnessed by the thirsty and the hungry.
You know I would have kept plodding onward
just for the children who still ask even now *why.*
I gave to you the Elvis albums and the blue couch.
But it's all right now.
We know each other better.
I can thank you.

From Behind Lace Curtains

or sitting on front porch wicker
The neighbors watched

As she brought out tablecloths
Satin covered photo albums
White chiffon dress pearl embellished
Piled high over framed pictures
A book of Celtic tattoos
Videos in plastic sleeves
Quilts and blankets

A tangled mess heaped
on a king-sized mattress
In the center of the driveway

She lit a match at each corner
   — *This is so over.* —

A terrible black smoke signal
Rose straight up in the windless sky

Let It Go

Put down your pack
  That buckled bag strapped
  across your shoulders

It's not working anymore
  Gravity has shifted the rocks
  from the night meadow

The bag-piped song at dusk which
  squeezed your lungs to tears

Let it go

The once wild once young man
  who loved the breath of you

Let it go

The tiny It who bled away
  before you knew It had rooted
Or could have had a name

Let it go

Nye Beach Walk

I learned that the ocean wind can lick your face
Like a mean cat
Yet heal your wounds at the same time.

My Left Hand

I don't much mind getting older
except for the pain–
a new pinch here and there
or some faded ache which
can return with vengeance

Now it's my left thumb–
cartilage in the base joint is gone
Doc says it could be fused
I just might do that
I'm losing my grip anyway
on pickle jars, weeds, memory

My left had is where my fourth finger lives
the one that used to have a silver band
with a diamond solitaire

Once when the man who gave it to me
came home drunk and soiled
that stone fell out the very next day

I saw it in the green shag carpet
As far as I know
It's still there glittering

Guadalajara Bus Station

In the path of the occasional passengers walking
along the wide sidewalk lay a yellow dog, mature
coyote size, dozing in a slant of sun. Regular breath
moved his ribs. His ears flickered. His top eyelid
opened and closed. Travelers passed the sprawling dog
taking care to not brush him with shoe or rolling suitcase.
The sun rose higher. The dog sighed, rolling over
to catch shifting sun beams. He was not a pup
nor was he old. He was a typical young
unemployed male, a good-for-nothing charmer.
Two people paused, murmuring endearments to him
deciding he might need food. The yellow dog stood,
stretched his hind legs one at a time, sniffed and
turned his head, refusing their offer of bread.
He lay down, stretching full length across the
sunny geographic middle of the walkway.
People continued to smile at his obstruction
while stepping around him.
He was perfectly capable of moving.
He was not begging for handouts.
He followed the sun.

NGU

The red work-truck's engine roared and charged
driven by the young man with a wild grin,
black hair and beard, and merry brown eyes,
who lived to log the forest.
NGU was hand-painted in white
on the doors and tailgate.
I had to ask.
"Never Give Up," he said.
He had no bumper stickers
shouting the slogans of other loggers.
No "Spotted Owls for Breakfast" or
"Log Now, Ask Later."

Alone in a fern-drenched grove
of old-growth Doug Fir,
he used his own gun to shoot himself.
If only he had read his sign
one more time.

In Seven Seconds

There occurred a disturbance
in the flow of air
not quite a sound
more a perception
of soft on soft

I turned to glimpse a sparse
confetti cloud
of floating white feathers

On the ground beneath
a mass of bird body
motionless but for one writhing wing
Moving closer, I defined two birds
of whites and darks

One young hawk grasped a stunned western thrush
its wings mantling over the thrush
slashing the breast
with a thorn of beak

The hawk dragged the thrush
as large as the raptor itself
under the laurel tree skirts
in three quick hops

A slaying so swift, silent, startling.

Territory

Spring rain washes
the west view windows

Reflective battlefields
for Western Thrush and Robins

Yet another wings at full speed
To fight a mirrored male

He loses in the first second of round one

Meanwhile the lusty Woodpecker
drums the hell out of the metal chimney cap

He calls it Victory

Downwinders from Hanford Nuclear Facility

He scrubbed his salt-sweat skin on a July day
Soaped palms gliding over thigh and groin

An odd bump there in the flex was
Still there the next day and the next

A nagging voice of dismissal rose above
A buried memory of his mother's first symptoms

A second lump sent him to the physician
You say your family lived downwind?

X-ray Machine, a Personal History of Radiation

I learned about bones early at the Buster Brown shoe store.
I inspected my own feet in the X-ray machine, which was
covered in smooth wood and made for children. Just push
the button and look as toes wiggled in a green glow—
a string of tiny toys in odd shapes.

We were supposed to wait until our shoes were on then
check for toe room, but my sister and I took turns as fast as
we could. We took our sox off spread toes wide and played
we were like monkeys. We discovered that hands fit into
the slot, too.

Davy the shoe man sat at the back of his special stool with
a sloping front on which a sliding metal cup was attached
to measure length and width. He always laughed and
tickled our feet. Davy said we were growing just about
right. And then we had more X-rays to make sure our toes
had wiggle room.

All of a sudden, at back-to-school time, the X-ray machine
was gone. How could we tell if our shoes fit? Davy pinched
my shoe's toe tip to make sure I had room to grow.

New brown and white saddle shoes carried me skipping
and hopscotching through the school year. We learned
about the Communist Threat and the atom bombs that
Russians had aimed at our towns. All the school children
practiced how to be safe from The Bomb with "duck and
cover," a quick maneuver to shelter under our desks. We
would be safe from Russian radiation.

• • •

On Viewing a Documentary Film at Los Alamos

The hush became total and dark

The narrator's perfect voice boomed
into the small theater

Familiar images of mushroom clouds
blossomed

Brilliant minds created the bomb here—
here on this high desert
here in this pristine town with
dry clear sun so bright
it made you blink

On film young white kids practiced
　　Duck and Cover
darting under wood school desks
　　　　grinning—aw c'mon
They knew it was a drill

Fast forward to grey images of
Hiroshima and Nagasaki
Miles of flattened scorched humans

No duck and cover there

The Japanese Tour Group was silent.

A Spinning in the Heart

1.
Search for an English word—
one single encompassing word
to capture the essence
of heat in an angry fist or
the flash of spring's first daffodil
Or catch of breath after a close call
  on icy stairs.
Find just one word for
the look in your old dog's eyes
    when he will no longer eat.

2.
Search for an elegant English word
equal to the Spanish "duende."
That one word holds the power of flamenco
and of Goya and the coral-striped sunrise.

That which elevates the emotions to flare
from soles of the feet,
That which causes the throat to tighten
tears to form, knees to tingle
the hair to rise on the scalp.
Duende.

3.
Search for a single Cambodian word for depression.
They know it as "the water in my heart has fallen."
Edging the Killing Fields are people
who feel "a spinning in the heart."
Search for their word to capture anxiety:
The people say "wind attacks"
as the breath struggles in and out
while the heart tumbles like falling stone.

● ● ●

Let Us Explain How This Happened in Your School, Sandy Hook, December 14, 2012

It happened because the mother was odd
  and the boy was weird
because the neighbors did not bake cookies to greet them
  blank curtains were drawn and lawns were wide

because the mother could no longer sing the boy to sleep
because the mother didn't lock the safe or hide the key
because the other kids squirted glue inside his locker

It happened because the mother took the boy to practice
because the mother took the boy Christmas shopping
because America sells mega-magazines everywhere
  and Hollywood sells video violence

It happened because of Gun Luv
because we are the land of the brave and the free
  and cowboys and *Bonnie and Clyde*
because bullets open doors to entry
because the boy didn't need to reload much

It happened because the NRA
  speaks louder than you and me
because there was no good guy with a gun
  to shoot the bad guy with a gun

It happened because we fail to be horrified for long
because hunters of quail and rabbit are silent

because reasonable people find no reason to be so

It happened because we have forgotten the poems
  we once knew by heart

A Gratitude

Today I ate a perfect summer-ripe peach
with baby-fine fuzzed skin

Along the cleft I sliced all around
then held it in both hands
and twisted

The peach split with a slight suck
into two hemispheres
one clutching a rugged pit

With the edge of my knife I peeled
chunks of rosy skin maps
leaving only flesh of the fruit
moist in my palm
glistening pale
to be sliced into quarter moons
and arranged on a blue plate

Six Haiku

spruce boughs heave and lift
in the storm like great green wings
of tethered captive birds

under the rose bush
speckled wrens scratch and cheep
sounds of quick kisses

the night sky river
powdered with stars and planets
elegant in black

lazy as a summer river
I cat-curl into you
sweet smiling Cheshire

the cello's swollen
belly let fly notes with wings
and angel halos

floating ship's roster—
Captain Sinker, Mr. Gale,
Major Storm on board

Blessing the Non-religious
May primary 2016

A crooked printed sign holds
the messy message of his cardboard life:
"Hungry–need gas money."

I stopped to give him an extra coffee and a couple of bills.
The guy bestows God's blessing upon me.
I smile and let that pass.
Today I feel great pleasure that my vote
for President went to an elderly, secular Jew
with a half-halo of white cotton candy hair.

Vignette of the Future

Early morning, sleepy eyed, I shuffle to the kitchen,
my back spasm twisting me to the left,
pain stabbing to my right leg.
He says something about the sun. There is no sun.
I ask *what about the sun?*
He says *I heard the sun a little while ago.*
You actually heard the sun? I ask, amazed at his powers,
trying hard to be agreeable.
*I mean I **saw** the sun,* says he, distracted by basketball
scores.
It was peeking under the clouds.
I look at grey sky, mist turning to drizzle.
I limp a little going around the corner to the sink.
You may have to help put my socks on today, I comment.
Whaaaat? It's not time to change, he shoots back.
It sure is, I retort. *How often do you change yours?*
Every six months he says, *on schedule with the alarm
batteries.*
I glare. *Did you hear what I said?*
He says *I heard you say something about changing the
clocks today.*
Later we laugh and he rubs my feet.

• • •

My Oregon Coast Journal Entry, Nov. 22, 2014

Something off-season
is happening in my garden–
Buds bulge on the iris stalks
clenching concealed yellow ruffles
These will never bloom

My first Christmas card has arrived
with a handwritten letter
from an old soulmate
who may not live
to see the solstice shift the light

But the Camellias have flared
into extraordinary early color,
coral blossoms clashing with baskets
of rusty-orange Mums

What's missing today is news
with more than a footnote
to observe Kennedy's assassination
the national memory of which has softened
as do worn denim jeans, washed,
zipped, palm-smoothed,
placed farther back on the shelf

Yet in a timely manner
when hummingbirds appear
seeking mild temperatures
I know the Coast Range
feels the sting of new frost

Tell me something I want to know

Tell me you had a full night's sleep

That you got out of bed and walked your dog
      as sunlight laced the tree tops

That you hungered, you cracked eggs
      whisked them with gleaming wire
      cooked them in bubbling butter

Wrap this story in fresh unmarked butcher paper
    No folds   no fat   no blood

Send it to me

I will receive it with hands which now
      look like my grandmother's

I will hold your story
      in the warm pulp of my palms
      nested as a trembling bird
      which I know has wings

Telephone Connection: Information Please

I leave a silent spot for you to place
an answer, to make some response

I comment about weather
the health of your dog
your aged electric fuse box
brakes on your car

Easy responses, one would think—
not too personal, not too demanding
The pauses grow longer
Still I leave the space for you to fill

The flow of words starts   halts   starts
You begin with local weather
Your dog threw up bird feathers
The repair bill was only $59
The brakes still grip

You planted the Japanese Maple

Then I knew your day went well
That your dog sleeps at your side

That you want to live

Takers

I've become one of those Takers
as in: one no longer adding
to the federal tax pie chart.

I'm old enough to kick back
and take some rewards
after decades of work
rising at 5 year after year.

I take my coffee to sip
for half the morning
And I take it with cream.
I shuffle into my slippers
should I choose to take that path.

So I take my time
though less of that remains.

I take a nap without asking
"Is it time to take a nap?"

I take up my book to read
after midnight.

I own these moments.
I'm taking them.

I Know About These Things

How my hand feels from the warmth of a dog
The whisper of a cat's tail curled around my knee
The vapor rush from the mouth of a coffee bag

I know about white gloves and satin slippers
a ripped hemline and a stained dress
I know how some people are separated only
by the width of a communion wafer

I know how I leaned on the fence as would a peony
against the rim of a vase
I have seen how a bouquet of black tulips became
a murder of purple ravens

At the Film Festival

Out of the darkness
  a three-year-old speaks his truth loudly:
"I want to see a different movie."
Soon, the film hiccups and stops.
The boy yells with delight:
"Uh Oh!"
How different it might be
  if we could choose our own life movie—
The beginning, the middle,
  and the finishing flourish with a power outage
  staying strong all the way home.

    ~Finis~

Priorities

Epigraph
For Nathaniel and Cimarron

"I'm here on the ER Gurney
  waiting for a room."
But what he worries about is his young dog –
His companion, his confidant, his lifeline.
"I have a dog sitter for tomorrow, but then
  I need to make a long-term plan."
He means a plan for his dog
  as the tumors have plans for him.

• • •

Squeezing Bees

I heard your hard cry
  found you waving your chubby fist
your fingers opened
you were squeezing a bee.

I plucked the stinger then
  iced your swollen hand.
I held you, my beautiful baby
  rocked you finally asleep.

I know you still squeeze bees
  with both your hands, child,
  silent fountains behind your eyes.

Relax your fists, child,
  unclench the stingers
  open your palms
  let the bees fly free.

Undoing.

Unseemly, unbanded, unwedded
Unappreciated, unhinged, unheard
Unkissed, unseen, undressed
Unmoored, unwrapped, unsure
Unable, unattached, unbonded
Underhanded, uncorrupted

Disbanding, dissolving, distressed
Disappeared, dissembling, disturbed
Disillusioned, disengaged, disconnected

Non-refundable, non-exchangeable, non-negotiable
Noncoherent, nonapproving, nonchalance
Nonessential, non-partisan, nonfiction
Nonissue, nondeductible
Noncontributory,
Nonorgasmic,
Nonaddictive, nonsense, nonfatal

Unmanned, unladylike, unchained
Unbecoming, uncooperative, unemotional
Unenforceable, unsung, undeterred
Ungirdled, unbridled

Orphaned

A child without parents is an orphan.
There is no noun for the opposite grief.
I reworked the order of departure
   once you said that you would not be here
   to take away my car keys.
You—the receptacle of my body's
   calcium to construct your bones and teeth.
My folate, iodine, and proteins to ensure your brain.
The milk I drank, the eggs I ate,
   those few glasses of wine,
   the smoke from your father's cigarettes—
You got all that, too.
You got the genes, both the good, and also the very bad.
I am so sorry for those.

My Daughter:
The Quickening

A gossamer wing
Fluttered in my womb's blood nest
Earthquake in my heart

My Daughter:
Chemotherapy, Week 6

Clumps of falling hair clot the brush
Don't throw it away, she says
Put it over there
Over there in that shrub
For the nesting birds
Next spring

The Thought of You

The thought of you
    taps my shoulder with a soft finger tip,
    or sometimes brushes my arm
    like a breeze slipping under the sill.
I hold the thought of you as I walk the hem of these
foothills.

Possibility

Unfinished poems lie like
    eggs in a nest.
There is a great possibility
    of hatchlings.

Cynthia Jacobi lives on the Oregon Coast where she is a visual artist as well as a poet.

She served on the Board of Directors for Writers on the Edge, and the Northwest Poets' Concord.

She is a member of Oregon Poetry Association, where she has won several awards for her poems, and Willamette Writers. As a Friend of William Stafford, Cynthia organizes a celebration of annual birthday readings at the Newport Library.

Her poems have been published in *Verseweavers*, *Tuesday*, and most recently, *Mortality Poems* and *The Grace of Oregon Rain.*

Jacobi presents reminiscences from a certain age, familiar yet fresh, capturing a culture that speaks to all generations. Reflections shimmer with humor, mercy, forgiveness, frailties – the entire human experience. Vivid sight, sound, and taste details weave evocative images full of emotion and metaphor. The poet's grand reflection says it best: "So I take my time /though less of that remains /…I own these moments /I'm taking them."--Catherine Rickbone, author of *Labyrinth Dance* and *What She Knows*.

When Cynthia Jacobi claims "I Know about These Things" I believe her. This compelling collection of personal poems starts with childhood and moves forward to imagining very old age. In the title poem she knows "How my hand feels from the warmth of a dog" and in poems about oranges or peaches, she helps us taste them with her. You will enjoy spending time with this caring and observant poet.
--Penelope Scambly Schott, Recipient of Oregon Book Award for Poetry and author of *On Dufur Hill*

Jacobi weaves her words into poems using old photographs, events, and stories as well as her own lived experiences, all of which pull at the readers' emotions and imagination, drawing them in to deeply feel each poem. Her words paint images of life that remain vivid despite the passage of time. She tells the truth, her truth. Indeed, she does know about these things.--Anita Janis

www.ingramcontent.com/pod-product-compliance
Lightning Source LLC
LaVergne TN
LVHW051706080426
835511LV00017B/2753